Duncan Bush
The Flying Trapeze

SEREN

Seren is the book imprint of
Poetry Wales Press Ltd.
57 Nolton Street, Bridgend, Wales, CF31 3AE
www.serenbooks.com
Facebook: facebook.com/SerenBooks
Twitter: @SerenBooks

The right of Duncan Bush to be identified as
the author of this work has been asserted in accordance
with the Copyright, Designs and Patents Act, 1988.

ISBN: 978-185411-572-0

A CIP record for this title is available from the British Library.

The publisher acknowledges the financial assistance of the Welsh Books Council.

Cover photograph © Spencer Dixey

Printed in Bembo by Berforts Group, Stevenage.

Author's website: www.duncanbush.com

The Flying Trapeze

for A

Contents

ONE

TWO

THREE

FOUR

ONE

The Young Man on the Flying Trapeze

Something appealing in these five-legged
man-headed portal bulls in the B.M. hallway,

their folded-back wings fledged like olivetrees.
The date-palm trunk's bark's

diamond-checked like a pistol-grip
and the snarling she-lion's stuck

with spears as an orange is with cloves.
And the men, with their square astrakhan beards,

hair of braided skeps
and Sphinxes' smiles, such calm

they have, such unemphatic authority
in their eyes and lifted hands – all gone

with Ashurbanipal and his lion hunts,
the neat incomprehensible cuneiform,

and god-built Nineveh
an allotment-dig of reddish dust.

Seventy thousand Assyrians left, Saroyan said,
but that in 1933 and the young man

in his story learning to cut hair in San Francisco,
half the city out of work: an Assyrian

not yet last of a once-great people
now alive one at a time, himself the whole race.

Couch Grass

Slow green fire,
shaggy pelt
of the plot's neglect,

each shock-haired
tussock levered loose
with the fork-prongs

rough-edged
enough to crisscross
your palms with cuts.

Gloved you straighten
shaking soil,
Perseus brandishing

the Medusa head
like a trophy scalp.
Tossed, it hisses

in the bonfire's yellow
smoke. Underground
it's already rife

as new rumour in deltas
of knotted fibres,
coarse white jointed net

that will spread
choking
the earth

if not the Earth
aswing
in its old string bag of meridians.

Ruskin and Millais and Effie and Rose

No one, least of all his bride of hours,
ever knew what took place
between John Ruskin's manly sideburns
that traumatic wedding-night.

Did he behold un-nymphlike pubic hair
– or menstrual blood?
The *vagina dentata*
of his mid-Victorian nightmares?

Years later – marriage annulled
for non-consummation,
Effie gone to Millais, Rose La Touche
dead, and the accelerating

downslope wobble to madness begun –
he drew *Moss and wild strawberry*,
as ever from nature: mossy mounds
soft-tangled as finches' nests,

and tiny tooth-edged strawberry trefoils
spilling unfruited
from the dark-cleft, back-sprawled,
unmistakably voluptuous rock.

Abandoned Orchard

It had long grown to rank savannah,
all summer a tangle of waist-tall
seeded grass, of umbellifers and bramble,
neglect and nesting birds.
There were always bullfinches and whitethroats,
and chiffchaffs like headlice in the topmost leaves.
One day I saw a hawfinch there,
saw it plain
on a blackthorn branch,
confirmed it in the circle of my binoculars.
And it became an orchard in allegory.
It was the garden of fallen apples.
At the end of October
I filled both side-pockets
with walnuts I could reach from the verge
outside, stretched at tiptoe,
fingertips loosing each one
out of the gaped green case.
We ate them at Christmas.
Pinned to the lintel
was a spray of mistletoe cut at dusk
on the shortest day
from an outhanging branch of an old appletree
abloom with it. I smeared the pearls
in the groin-crease
of my own appletree, wondering if the seed –
embryonic, nucleate, ungraspable as frogspawn
in its semen-whitish jelly –
needed to pass
through a missel-thrush's gut first.
I know. I was trying to get back (as they say) to
what I'd never known but hoped
we'd bought into: a life simplified,

a sequence of moments
distilling
to a bead
of ancient honey
out of early retirement,
the bee-swarm clustering among a ratrace of prices
for country properties
and the greying, childrenless late fifties.
Which is why I liked to think, as I still do
when I walk past his orchard
– its rot-collapsed goose-ark,
the gate-bolt rusted hard into its keep –
of the long foresight of this man
whoever he was
(and who never comes there now)
who bought or didn't sell for building
that sloping end acre of pasture
all those years ago, and enclosed it
and planted his trees well-spaced
in grass mown back to tousled lawn to sit out on
on summer weekends
for all the fruit he'd never pick or eat.

Cider Orchard Story, near Pershore: Verbatim

"So this old boy come past as we was scrumping apples
off this tree, like. I must have been about ten, eleven.
This branch was hanging down outside,
I mean we didn't even have to go over for em.
I took one bite out of one and spit it out. Yeuuch!
I mean it looked a beauty. Beautiful red skin, like.
And the like flesh this lovely white, so you could see pink
like staining back into the teethmarks.
Like you had something wrong with your gums,
aye. That ginger vitus.

"Anyway, like I say, this old boy come past.
He never said nothin. Jus' looked at us.
'Bit sour, i'n they,' he said, just like that. And made a face,
like he must have tried one himself.
'A bit,' I said. 'Aye,' he said. He stood there,
looked at me. Then he laughed. One of them laughs
it's half a cough with all the, like, phlegm.
'You silly young bleeders,' he said. 'Them's not eaters,
them's drinkers.' I never said nothing. I looked at him.
I thought he was a, you know, nutcase.
So he laughed again and carried on
up the road, laughing and coughing.

"So we tries a few more. We only works out after
what the old cunt was on about, yeah."

Interregnum, near Worcester

Flat sun's slant hazy
On the wood's full crowns: August's
Days gleam mellower,

Melancholy, light
Of Summer tainted with first
Gold of September

While these thick-leaved oaks
Look braided, flat, archaic
As old tapestry –

Trees a fleeing king
Hid in, clutching his kingship
Like a bowling-ball.

Sudden Death of An Acquitted Suspect in a Gangland Killing

For a full decade of his adult life
they'd talked about him
out of earshot,
and he'd loved it.
But without new rumour
memories grow short.

No one missed him
in the boozers, lunchtime.
And all that afternoon
he was an unnoticed absence
in what the papers called
his usual haunts:
the betting-shop,
the barber's.

He'd planned to put a monkey
on a horse. It looked a cert.
And then, he thought,
he'd drop in for his weekly trim.

The horse lost. His place
in the wait for the chair
went to a fat boy
who asked for a David Beckham.

As for the money, that
had changed hands long ago
to show the deed was done,
as old scores are settled
before bodies are ever found.

A Blood Rose

"The one who will love you for life
You must first stab once to the heart."
- I dreamed this proverb last night
Out of the bitter male romanticism

Of the old Buenos Aires districts
Where a duel of knifeblades
Refined the bullfight, and long before
Football rooted in cracks in tribal streets

And violence was even more stylish
And brutal, and when in praise and
Lamentation of its murderous grace
The tango flowered from trios

In the back of those cafe-bars
Looking on at the man in black
Trousers cut so tight his sex
Must be taped pointing upwards

And a woman with hair long unshorn
But drawn so close to the skull
You cannot dream the dark
Cascade of its unpinning...

So you look on instead at this
Couple, in the perpendicular act of
Consummation which the tango is
When danced utterly

By a woman you want and a man
You cannot emulate, your single
Consolation that duende is, like jealousy,
A gift from the watched to the watcher.

Duende Tango

South, far south of old Durango.
South again. El mundo? Fango.
No one trips the light fandango.

Not sure if you can't or can go?
Costive? (mescal, owls' eggs, mango...)
Loosen up with a duende tango.

Tired of art under the quango?
Busk like Schnittke? Strum like Django?
Change your tune. Play the duende tango.

Sick of pimping to the dollar
Like the junta's ayatollah?
Sport an ultra-violet collar.
Knife-fights. Football. Piazzolla.

On Being Anthologised

It may select the best but somehow just
brings out the worst in us, the Lifeboat
Mentality: relief, first, that we're *in*,

but then, increasingly, eyeing of others and
the envious unforgivable maths – so many
poems from one already lionised, so few

of our own – like counting heads
and lifejackets silently, rationing water
by estimate cupfuls

in the full of the sea with the bitter
condolence that not all who escape
a sinking survive the lifeboat,

and hope – still – of the passing cruise-ship
"Luck" or "Belated Discovery", or a longer solo pull
to that dark cypress-isle Posterity...

And so, with a last mantra-mutter
at our lips about First being Last
and Last being First in some

future beyond our own, hunched,
croak-dry, hoarding a sodden blanket
in the bilges, we're already going down.

In Memory of Basil Bunting

"Ignore the critics", Basil Bunting advised,
the day I interviewed him. "And never respond
to reviews, especially good ones". He was spry
in his old-gold waistcoat and professorial beard.
He wrote *Briggflatts* and lyrics of a delicate
beauty, but much in draft was balled for bin or grate.
And so he died, in his parents' Quaker faith in
the dignity of held silence amid the drab
paucities of old age on a state pension, and a sense
that the careers of glib paravails – hyperactive
mediocrities and untiring networkers,
website hitmen or other stars of lowest
magnitude who know that poetry is just one
more branch of publicity – bloom in a rummage
of printed matter fit only for grasping in
an outside lavatory built over a lime-pit.

A Provincial Affair

Tolstoy relates somewhere the story of
an army officer who is stationed
for a short time in a remote province,
one of those bucolic postings with which
Russian literature is richly furnished.
In the usual course of things in provincial life,
he is invited to soirées
at a local landowner's house, and
becomes a regular visitor.
A friendship develops with his
host's daughter, and they find they have much
in common, so that each looks forward more and
more to his next visit. Before long
they're in love, though neither speaks of it
or shows any sign of these feelings. She
is an innocent and unworldly girl
who mistakenly thinks herself plain; he
has always been afflicted with shyness.
Despite this, their relationship deepens,
and if circumstances had only stayed
as they were it was inevitable
that in time, through a word or look or touch,
their love would have been revealed. Then one day
the officer receives a new posting,
to another distant part of Russia.
The time comes for him to attend his last
evening at the landowner's house, prior
to departure early next morning. He
and the young woman are compelled to spend
their whole evening in the company of
the other guests, though each agonises
to be alone with the other. At last
they find themselves a moment together
in the hallway, as the officer is
preparing to leave. He has
only to speak his feelings, take her hand.
She will respond, their love for each other

will be made known, and all will be well. But
he is stifled by shyness again,
and she too is unable to utter
a word of what is oppressing her heart.
They utter their goodbyes politely, and he leaves.
Tolstoy tells us that if this encounter
had only been resolved
differently two people would have found
joy and companionship, enough to last into old age. Instead
the officer lives his life a bachelor, and spends
his whole career at different army posts;
the woman lives and dies at home, unwed.
Both had squandered their hope of happiness
for the sum of their lives merely because,
when the chance to do so was there, neither
found the courage to speak their true feelings.
This parable has always haunted me.

Lahore

Inside every army is a crowd trying to get out.

Inside every crowd is a mob close to panic.

Inside every mob is an unconvinced suicide.

Inside every suicide is a tarnished spoon.

Inside every spoon is a world the wrong way up.

Inside every world is a demagogue's drum.

Inside every drum is a marching army.

Inside every army is a crowd struggling to get out.

And that's how the waters come down at Lahore.

TWO

The Rom Out of Romania

For some reason I always
noticed it: *Manouche je t'aime.*
Gipsy I love you
spray-canned on the pillar of a motorway bridge

near Lille, that drab post-industrial border where
French meets Flemish in place-names
impenetrable as code. Years it was
there, for anyone to read.

Some girl, I thought,
and a boy who worked once for a touring fair,
jeans too tight, a metal comb
showing in a back pocket,

cigarette-packet furled into his t-shirt sleeve
up by the bicep.
A boy who'd swing himself
as if on stepping-stones

across the floor,
dodgem-car to swirling dodgem-car,
riding the sparking poles under the chicken-wire
to screaming girls,

push-starting them off
when they crashed or the current died.
She's married now, I thought,
with a kid and a dirty cooker,

but'll drive back sometimes
to see her mother, and go past it again
in the broken whine of traffic,
one of the maybe millions who've read it

who for a second or two
in the long boredom of motorways
all have their own sense of what it means
to love Manouche

so you have to squirt his name in fluorescent
paint on concrete – but not Manouche,
he's moved on too,
to another country, real cars

which ran dead at the roadside
or were left a winter
in an orchard in the rain.
His father gossipped to his horses in the Romani,

but Manou', he's got a different touch,
and a curse is anyway the only word
for a car not even yours.
He's got a mobile home

with its axles up on concrete blocks
in a mud-tracked field of old Fiats, Ladas, Skodas –
horse-power junked and rust-edged
but which, if anybody can, he'll

somehow get to spark, re-spark, start again.

East Side Story

1. *Was gibt es Neues?*

Berlin-Ost's rebuilding: tungsten-toothed saw-whine
loud from hallways of poured concrete: kerb,
pave-stone, marble tiling cut and laid to line

to refloor old workers' blocks bulldozed for
showroom shopping. Meanwhile, hard-faced Poles
in earflap hats, eyes tight as buttonholes,

or men out of some further, rawer, darker
East – Khazhak or Chechen or Serb –
busk Cold War militaria and tourist kitsch

in a tundra wind under the Brandenburg gate –
they'd hawk each other's mother
wife and daughter for a chance of getting rich.

The latest babushka doll's a Yeltsin drunk –
creased eyes, silver quiff, all phoney yo-ho-ho;
inside him is Gorbachov – that balding, birth-marked pate;

then – face like a frost-corrupted swede –
Brezhnev; and, next size down, a dinky Uncle Joe...
Last, inmost and tiniest of this bear's litter

of hardliners or tools, the bearded Lenin, shrunk
from the gigantism of his civic statuary
to the runt. (All five for *"Zwanzig Mark, bitte!"*)

2. *Wiedersehen macht Freude: Ina's Story.*

"The flat I grew up in had Vladimir Ulyanov slavic-cheeked,
heroic on the wall, and looked over The Wall
at neighbours we ignored, spied on, envied, feared.

The sills were crumbling and the plumbing leaked;
but now that building's rubbled, cleared –
gone forever like the type of chocolate or soap

we had when I was young. So childlike, crude
those coloured wrappers... how ingenuous our hope
in this untwinned half-city under siege where all

commodities were basic, every brand the only choice.
My parents were Professors, Party members who'd
mugged Russian (fluent in the Party's voice).

Too old to pick up English, now they beg or hustle
part-time classes in drab suburbs, each paid hour
the gift of brusque incomers with degrees from

Bonn or Stuttgart, Audis and academic muscle.
My father's old age is graffiti muttered, but unwritten;
the past a souvenir hunk of concrete walling bitten

off and gnawed till it's sharp dust.
All day he turns this cud, daren't spit it out,
but cannot swallow it – although he knows I must.

Berlin, 1998.

A Season in Sarajevo

This, then, is the Book of Hours
Amidst green marrows and bean-flowers,
Wisteria and thyme,
The parked car sticky from a shedding lime.

This, now, is the Book of Days,
Of coffee-rings and heat haze,
The old ladder left in a cherry tree
And the bias-wheeled hospital trolley.

And this must be the Book of Lives,
The larval dead in their celled hives
And the jay on the lawn
Burying its acorn.

Still Living at Sixteen

Like many Luxemburgers he
was (as they say) of farming stock.
   Meaning (as they don't say) he was
a generation and a few
   sold fields from a peasant, belly
and brain. His land was the living
   left him. He'd never worked it – or
perhaps even walked it, the full
   length of it. I never saw him
walk anywhere except to his
   Merc or that old van he drove. What
it was was 23 hectares
   of good grazing at the edge of
a village. I imagine it
   was just flat fields to him when his
grandfather died and left him them.

   That was in 1988.
But Luxembourg was growing in
   wealth and population, many
of the incomers highly-paid
   employees of the new E.U.
institutions or of the banks
   and finance houses (the old tale –
nothing makes money like money).
   And the result of all this was
a housing boom; and this village
   was convenient to drive to
the city from. So, like many
   Luxemburgers, he sold his land
for building. His one big regret
   later was that he didn't wait

a few more years before selling
in what was a strongly upward
    seller's market: we'd rented the
house next door to his, and he told
    me so in French poorer than mine.
He re-stated this on later
    occasions, ruminative, sour,
as if the error or loss still
    plagued him. Despite what seemed to me
the immense sum – all profit – he'd
    got from the sale, he never moved
from the drab, cheaply-built 'Fifties
    house which had been his parents'
and was almost identical
    to ours. A bigger house, bigger
garden, didn't interest him, nor

    did an apartment in town. This
house in this village was all he
    had known, so it was all there was.
But he talked about his money
    often, this huge sum he'd made and
the huger sum he might have had
    by waiting, as if still unsure
whether to boast or admit his
    own stupidity. Sometimes he
got in his car and drove over
    and toured the streets of the costly
new dormitory suburb they'd built
    on the 23 hectares he'd
sold. He even told me what all
    those houses were worth now, jointly.
He'd worked out the prices, added

them all up, and it embittered
him, as if the developer,
    a Portuguese like most of those
who do building work or other
    manual jobs in Luxembourg, had
somehow hoodwinked him by buying
    the ground in 1989
at a 1989 price.
This was the only thing that seemed
    to harrow what could justly be
called a placid and equable
    temperament. His eyes were only
slightly less blue and unperplexed
    than a doll's, and he had thinning
hair, worn long when we first moved there
    but now shaved to ginger stubble.

    Luxembourg is a small country
famous for three things: cheap booze, cheap
    cigs, cheap petrol. And I suppose
these represented my neighbour's
    vices fairly, at least those in
plain view. Drinking, smoking, eating,
    then driving to the supermarket
for more of the same was his life.
    My wife tells me that I'm sometimes
ungenerous in my view of
    other people, and perhaps by
now that's obvious. But the truth
    is, it was hard to give his life
a favourable or useful slant.
    One day he must have decided,
though, to cultivate an outside

interest, because he started
hoarding scrap. I call it scrap, but
    Luxembourg was officially
by now the richest country in
    the world per capita, having
overtaken Switzerland. And
    the citizens of this tiny
nation's sense of self-worth and
    prosperity was expressed – how
else? – by shopping. And not just for
    more booze, cigs, petrol, food, but white
. goods, televisions, furniture,
    lawnmowers, barbecue ovens
and patio accoutrements...
    And, when a brand-new item was
purchased, the old one it replaced

    was put out on the pavement. What
you threw away became a
    status symbol of its own – one
more public even than the new,
    expensive thing you'd just bought but
probably liked to keep indoors.
    Conspicuous consumption draws
its second breath on ostentatious
    waste. Each commune had collection
days for these *objets encombrants*
    or large domestic items, and
my neighbour had ringed all the dates.
    There was this bearded friend he drank
with, and they roamed the area
    in his old white van on all the
designated days. People tend

to place things out for collection
the night before, so they'd arrive
    at dawn, before the disposal
squad could get there; and whatever
    they fancied and could lift they'd load
into the van. The garden space
    behind his house became home to
all this junk: at first a sculpture
    park, then a full cemetery,
for whatever he picked up that
    looked reconditionable or
salvageable, anything from
    kiddies' bikes to old fridges, stoves
to lava lamps. When I looked at
    all this stuff it made me queasy,
the way too much of anything

    does. There wasn't one piece amongst
it all you'd go so far as to
    covet, let alone steal, but they
somehow seemed the kind of items
    only a society that
was as soft in the head as it
    was in the gut would simply throw
away. When I asked my neighbour
    about it, though, he claimed he was
mending things, or servicing them,
    then reselling them. Not that it
was a business, he made plain: he
    didn't need money. Not him.
This was a hobby, nothing more.
    And he made himself out to be
a champion of recycling. I

listened to him. But I saw more
coming in in the van each week,
   and nothing ever went out. And
though he tinkered at things I never
   saw him repair so much as a
punctured tyre, while his claims for the
   ecological benefits
seemed belied or contradicted by
   an entrepreneurial dream
that made him relate fantasies
   of potential resale profits
to me across our common fence.
   Meanwhile, my upper rear windows
looked out on a growing junkyard.
   The single consolation in
all this was that we didn't own

   the house we lived in, didn't have
to live next door to him forever,
   my wife, kids and I. But having
to look at all that clapped-out
   secondhand equipment grieved my
heart, and more I think than it could
   have gladdened his. But I have no
idea what gladdened his heart.
   He wasn't married, he had no
children, and his parents were dead:
   so it wasn't family. Some nights
he brought women to the house, late.
   Girls. They came with him in his car,
from, I imagined, bars in town
   where they will leave with you by some
arrangement if the facilities

on hand don't suit the customer.
I spoke to one once. She must have
    stayed overnight, because at eight
in the morning she came out on
    the pavement, where I saw her make a
quick, impassioned but slightly
    distracted call on her mobile.
Then she must have confused the two
    gateways because she wandered back
in through mine and passed out of sight
    from where I was craning to watch
at my front window. I walked through
    the bedrooms to a back window
in time to see her squatting by
    my hedge. Her skirt was so short she
didn't have to do much to piss

    on the ground except squat. I went
downstairs with a sort of furious
    rapidity, enabling me
to confront her on the path next
    to the house; but the outraged sense
of fury vanished when I looked
    into her face – what could she have
been? Sixteen? I spoke to her quite
    politely, in French, then German,
but she didn't understand. She
    spoke Kosovar, I guessed, or Croat –
or whatever they speak in those
    murderous states whose sole exports
then were gangsters and whores – and I
    ended up shrugging as if I
understood her confusion and let

her past. I never told my wife
of that meeting. Eventually
　　we moved, to another village,
to a house we were buying on
　　the usual mortgage contract, in
a quiet street. But my former
　　neighbour must still be there. At least,
when I drive through our old village
　　now I see the junk in Number
Sixteen's piling up even in
　　the garden at the front. As I've
said, he wasn't a man it was
　　easy to like or respect. But
then, those who are often turn out
　　to be unworthy of it, and
when I think of him now I can

　　see that at least there was a kind
of wistfulness in him, with his
　　adjustable wrench and that new
set of tube spanners he bought, and
　　the minutes he occasionally
spent tinkering with simple
　　machines he didn't understand –
this man wealthy enough to leak
　　away his life in a village
he'd never leave, and becoming
　　heavier-set every year but
with something in him still longing
　　for useful work, yearning for the
universality of a good
　　mechanic's skill on whatever
happens to come in the workshop.

L'Enfance de Rimbaud

1.

Saison de tristesse,
Coeur comme une ville que le cirque
N'a pas visitée.

2.

Dimanche éternel
De ces villes en province, même
Le cafard blafard.

Rimbaud's Childhood

1.

Season of Sadness,
Heart like a town the circus
Never visited.

2.

Eternal Sundays
Of these drab provincial towns,
Even the blues wan.

Douce France

Finest of all colours
which please me is the blue
with a violet tint in it

only ever glimpsed
going past
down some 'D' road in the Var

or the Meurthe-et-Moselle,
but more and more
rarely and each year

in fainter and patchier traces
as the hem of a robe
still glows

from crazing frescoes:
that matchless
blue

surrounding big
white
capitals

of the ancient
advertisement flaking away
on a gable-end of the first

or last house
in some near-derelict hamlet,
ferns in the guttering,

the word *DUBONNET*
itself now
almost

unreadable,
and something
surges back

in thoughts of all
the boys from these villages
gone

gone for soldiers,

each one

for a rifle
and a good wool overcoat,
for a farewell drink

at the first
ratatat
of the drumskin,

and all
this

all of it

wheat under the plough.

Douce France

De toutes les couleurs
qui me plaisent
la plus belle est un bleu

tirant sur le violet
qu'on n'entrevoit qu'en passant
sur quelque route départementale dans le Var

ou en Meurthe-et-Moselle,
mais de plus en plus
rarement,

tache fanée
pareille aux bords craquelés
de la robe luisante

d'une fresque: c'est le bleu outremer
sans pareil
à l'oeil

entourant les lettres
grandes et blanches
du vieux mot

de la réclame
sur le mur lépreux
de la dernière maison

d'un village abandonné
ou presque,
de la fougère dans les gouttières

et le nom de DUBONNET lui-même
presque illisible
et quelque chose reflue

quand on pense
à tous les garçons
de tous ces villages

partis

partis
en soldat, tous

pour un fusil
et un bon pardessus de laine
pour une coupe d'adieu

au premier coup
de la peau
du tambour

et tout cela

tout

du blé
pour la charrue.

Mitterand's Last Supper

Towards the end, when Uncle felt his last powers failing him
(and only he and God knew what his powers had been)
he telephoned a famous chef,
then invited his friends to join him for a farewell dinner
(though only he and they know who was asked to dine).
He had a prostate the size of an orange,
it was rumoured; also that one that large had been removed
(though only he and his doctors knew
the truth about his medical condition).
But Uncle's appetite that night was unimpaired.
First he gorged on oysters, *fines de claire*,
their bracing delicious scent of the sea and other wetnesses,
that deliquescent taste – sip-swallowing
dozen after dozen, desisting only at
the point of being sick. Next he'd ordered *ortolans*,
tiny speckled birds trapped in the Midi by flung nets
or lime-glued branches, and now roasted to a wizened gold.
He crushed each one into his figured napkin to inhale the odour
of its richness more deeply, then devoured it
– flight, song, body –
whole, in the traditional way,
swallowing the entrails and crunching the bones
in those slanted teeth that always looked like porcelain
(though only Uncle and his dentist knew the secrets of his teeth).
It was not a sombre evening. This was a night for old friendship
and steady self-indulgence as the courses came and went.
The company spoke of gossip and politics, sport and enemies,
culture, holidays and the fugacious comedy of sex
(but only they and the silent waiters could tell us what was said).
Finally a dessert was served, a dessert such as
can only be imagined (though only the chef is privy to
the recipe, which perhaps will never be repeated).

They broke up in the early hours
yet almost formally, each guest in turn
kissing and embracing Uncle for the last time as if
receiving another dignification at his hands,
or another whispered word. The waiters switched the lights on
and started to clear the table's disarray.
Bevelled mirrors repeated to infinity
the suddenly wearied majesty of rooms lit too late
and by too many bulbs. Outside, his friends dispersed,
keeping inviolate the evening's confidentialities.
And from that moment
neither food nor secrets crossed Uncle's lips again,
as he fasted without impatience
from the Fifth Republic into History.

La Cène de Tonton

Vers la fin, quand Tonton
sentit ses dernières forces l'abandonner
(et seuls lui et Dieu
savaient quelles avaient été ses forces)
il téléphona à un chef de renom
et puis convia ses amis
à partager un dîner d'adieu
(bien que seuls lui et eux sachent
qui on avait invité).
Il avait une prostate
grosse comme une orange, disait-on;
et qu'on lui en avait enlevé
une de cette taille-là
(mais seuls lui et ses médecins connaissaient
la vérité sur sa condition médicale).
En tout cas l'appétit de Tonton
Ne semblait pas avoir diminué.
D'abord il se goinfra d'huîtres
fines de claire −
leur odeur tonifiante et délicieuse
de la mer et d'autres choses mouillées,
ce goût déliquescent −
sirotant-engloutissant
douzaine sur douzaine et s'arrêtant
seulement sur le point de vomir.
Ensuite il avait commandé des ortolans,
de petits oiseaux grivelés
pris dans le Midi
au filet lancé ou à la glu
alors rôtis, couleur d'or ratatiné.
Il écrasa chacun
dans sa serviette gaufrée
afin d'inhaler au plus profond
sa riche odeur,
puis le dévora
- le vol, le chant, le corps -
entier, de la manière traditionnelle,
avalant les entrailles
et croquant les petits os
sous ses canines de biais

qui ressemblaient toujours à de la porcelaine
(bien que seuls Tonton et son dentiste
connussent les secrets de ses dents).
Ce ne fut pas une soirée sombre. Ce fut
une nuit pour la vieille amitié
et la gâterie
pendant que les plats se succédaient.
On parla de potins et de politique,
du sport et des ennemis,
de la culture, des vacances,
et de la comédie fugace du sexe
(mais seuls eux et les serveurs silencieux
pourraient nous dire ce qu'on avait dit).
Finalement on servit un dessert,
un dessert tel qu'on ne peut qu'imaginer
(car seul le chef en connaissait
la recette, qui ne sera
peut-être jamais répétée).
Ils se quittèrent au petit matin
mais presque protocolairement, chaque invité
à son tour embrassant Tonton
pour la dernière fois
comme s'il recevait de ses mains
une autre distinction
ou un message chuchoté. Les serveurs
allumèrent les lustres
et commencèrent à débarrasser
de la table le désarroi.
Des glaces biseautées repétèrent
à l'infini
la majesté soudain fanée
de salles éclairées trop tard
et par trop d'ampoules.
Dehors ses amis se dispersèrent.
Et à partir de ce moment-là
ni nourriture ni secrets ne franchirent plus
les lèvres de Tonton,
qui jeûnait sans impatience
depuis la Cinquième République vers l'Histoire.

Wear

The dull oil of use
On things long-disused stirs us
Obscurely: tool-hafts;

Lubricated parts
Of machines, piston-bright; coins
Handled smooth of face.

Wear delights the eye
Glutted with the new, the crass,
The disposable.

Even in Rome you note
Not St. Peter's mild gaze but
The patina of

Kisses yellowed on
His hallux, the bright strap to
That brazen sandal.

THREE

Golden Girl, 2000

Cathy Freeman stays cool, looks good.
(She'll win Gold in a fast canter,
still in her tracksuit hood.)

She crouches at her blocks
ad-sized up the whole side of a building
in downtown Sydney, near the Rocks.

Once one of the Stolen Generation,
now she queens the headlines
to "unite a sports-mad nation".

Meanwhile in this neon Kings Cross dive
five linked beer-rings on the counter
under the shouting tv ("Back Live")

kibitz Olympic glory through a haze
to the autochthonous Ocker male,
the solo drinker's toad-dull gaze

of someone going down with flu:
she's just one or another of these
lithe black girl athletes he'll later wank to.

Sydney, New South Wales.

Motel Pool Gossip Party

So, it was tacitly surmised, a not–
so-jolly rogering
in the end for the pale-lashed,
ginger-freckled, milk-skinned and

untannable tourist single (28 yrs.)
relieved of the bank-new
Australian notes in her purse and –
inconceivable not to speculate
– prior to that

of some hard-borne drought
of celibacy (though she brought
complaint
only of the former)

by the full-bearded, brawny,
teak-oil-brown
part-Aboriginal itinerant
backpacker

described by the taller of the
paired
Cairns policemen in pressed
uniform shorts
as "a known semi-feral"

whom she'd met at a public bench on the esplanade
and admitted to her room in the Sandy Cays
motel "for coffee", and who went

by the name – false no doubt, in all
but its fitting piratical edge –
of Henry Morgan.

Cairns, Queensland.

54

The Dreaming

Singleted, skinny-shanked, bare
soles dust-grey, with his termite beard
and ghost-far gaze he outsits the wattle-tree's shade,

a cloud-shape wheeling star-slow West to East
across the town park. Till tonight's drink
round a fire fed litter

a plastic Coca-Cola bottle refilled
at a municipal outside tap gets him across
the desert of the day.

Townsville, Queensland

Donald George Bradman, 1907-2001

I and Australia re-dreamed Don Bradman
on the night he died. Still young, a boy vignetted

in an old tinted cigarette-card photo enlarged
from a team grouping, he wore a dove-grey

club blazer with rose grosgrain edging
collar and lapels, the misty corrugated-iron stand

at Bowral or Goulburn behind him
on a day of heat and heaviness for a game against

a country side, his place in the XI not yet secure.
His eyes held that expression of appraisal neither

rueful nor pleasurable of a batsman with a brand-new bat
and its first run not the cracking

square cut or princely drive rehearsed
on the dressing-room's cleat-splintered deal planking,

just a firm clip beyond midwicket or a push
past cover from a ball not quite on off stump, a single

so easy you trot it, and after grounding the bat
at the bowler's crease you lift the blade

and scrutinise where the ball
has printed it with red and an arc of stitching:

that first mark it gets you off the mark with, sweat not
yet broken, all the records unknown, and intact.

FOUR

Fragonard's Lovers

Sundays in The Frick:
Deep-piled, dim-lit, a quiet
Not mortuary but

Mausoleum-like.
Here Fragonard's lovers live
Their garden idyll

Overshadowed by
Irreal, blue trees whose crowns
Swell anvil-shaped like

Summer thunder-clouds...
Mme. Du Barry, who once
Refused these paintings

(But never suave Louis!)
is bones; and old Mr. Frick,
Whose excellence of

Taste in art was fed
By wealth derived from whisky,
Coke and steel, is too.

Yet these rococo
Darlings of Fragonard's still
Entrance and enchant —

They move us with their
Infant-like impatience for
Uncertain joys. We

See there is no time
Beyond these instants for this
Flush-cheeked belle, her swain;

The roses are all
But overblown, and Cupid's
Asleep, bored by what

He foreknows in love's
Triumphal crowning with that
Wreath of fresh-cut blooms.

West 86th Street

A style I've always
Admired: that of elderly
Well-off Jewish men

Who live on New York's
Upper West Side, near the Park,
In tall apartment

Buildings with doormen
And foyers and residents'
Committees, and who

Wouldn't set a foot
On the sidewalk in winter
Without first donning

Solid Florsheim brogues,
A raglan-style overcoat
With dark fedora,

A tasselled wool scarf,
and taking tan leather gloves
(One unworn, and gripped

In the other): such
Prudent elegance – pausing
On their own porch step

To pull the second
Glove on and assess the day,
The street, the city.

Obituary Page

The classic photo:
Brown eyes, lids hooded, saurine;
The banded trilby

At an ad-man's tilt.
Saul Bellow died yesterday.
The rest move up one.

Avedon's Drifters

After wall on wall of
the important, fashionable or glamorous
– famed pictures of the famous –
in his last exhibition at the Met, it's unexpectedly

in the last gallery-space
that we confront
Richard Avedon's portraits
of sky-eyed losers –

these shrunken-bellied rueful old boys
dapper in Western-style duds,
or no-longer-youthful tumbleweeds
with a gleam of wildness not yet wholly dulled –

itinerants
encountered at obscure and remote
locations which are undepicted (each subject
framed against white, stark as for an ID shot)

but commemorated in all the poetry
and desolation
of a road-number, a named place
passed through once:

"Clarence Lippard, drifter,
Interstate 80, Sparks, Nevada, 1983";

"James Kimberlin, drifter,
State Road 11, Hobbs, New Mexico, 1980";

"Clifford Feldner, unemployed ranch hand,
Golden, Colorado, 1983";

"Alan Silvey, drifter,
Route 93, Chloride, Nevada, 1980":

lives gone awry in America, though each
in Whitman's words
was a child once
sleeping in his mother's bedroom.

And we are moved
by these faces, by their grievous
dignity, we are halted
in passing (see how scrutinising faces

among a queue-dense wet-Sunday public are
ennobled by sympathy,
by a troubled intentness
– this on the faces of urbanite Noo Yawkers

who in the pavement's flow ignore daily
and all week the sight
of other persons
adrift, deracinate or feral).

Yet something too shrinks back
at these photographs,
some diffidence or
delicacy,

since which of us could imagine singling out
each out-of-luck stranger
in a bar forecourt or at a roadside,
brokering the fee for the shots?

Perhaps in all human empathy,
all art, a ruthless prurience lies visible
like a watermark
at a certain angle to the light.

Either way, here on display,
in that moment's monochrome daylight
not harsh but printed
freckle-clear, pore-clear

and bigger than life-size
are these vagabond drinkers
or feckless workhands
whom ordinarily the tactful eye slides past,

undependable or disappointment-wounded
sons or husbands
of the fugitive kind, caught
before they edge away out of focus again:

guys of whom all their lives it was said
that they were never, ever there.

Richard Avedon, 1923-2004

Hellas

Old-gold glint of stubble into the sun,
the straw tedded all morning in rows by women
working in a line with wooden-toothed rakes,

cowled and all in black in the earth-crazing heat,
as if Greece through its widows still honoured
all the dead of Thermopylae or Troy,

these patches of scytheable land they left.
Now at noon the single fig-tree poises a shadow
wide as a cloud's on the empty field,

squared stones tumbled in dry-stalked thistles
at its foot, as from a broken wall or
dwelling older than Agamemnon's tomb,

though the roots long ago surmounted
building and builder. As the forking mounds a
dark seam in an ash-tree like a woman's crotch,

pagan, atavistic – twinned branches parted, smooth
and round as thighs – the fig-tree's eroticism is
ambiguous, polytheistic-perverse: green, the figs hang

asymmetrical, tight-pouched, testicular; only later,
darkened, ripening to a split, will each gape pink to
moist satin... Was it this aroused us,

brought us into its shade as inside a tent, though
nowhere to lie down except in dust and dead thistles.
so we stood instead, joined in that intent

staggering dance to ejaculation – the hug and
jounce of your legs as if shinning up me –
till I backed your weight half-seated

against the tree's low limb, limber in its give,
grunting with exertion and heat, half-blind with sweat
and dazzle through the shattering leaves, deaf

to stridulations of crickets, our own gasps and cries.
All through it, I was fearful of snakes, scorpions,
but we came back there next day too

as to a numinous site – oracle or spring or echo –
the lubricities of locus still compelling
but obscure. And where we'd pressed

against that horizontal branch – inner-tendoned
like a hurdler's outstretched thigh – we found
a snipped-off bunch of grapes, blue-bloomed,

laid there, we could only think, as an offering
by someone, man or woman, who'd seen us
shade-splashed, strenuous in that green cage of desire

down a field aglitter with gold where each leaf
was eyed, each tree marked a metamorphosis,
though in land where not every fig-tree fruited.

And when we'd again done what we'd come
there to do, out of profane joy of the earth
and in the lust of youth, we ate

some of the grapes and left the others for the god.

Telemachus

There was a seaweed-covered rock we swam out to
singly, to touch a hand to for a dare
at three-quarter tide
– a matted black pubic knoll

In the slow rise of the calm bay,
about to drown to a nest of bubbles,
become part of the eerie incoming underwater
queendom of eels

for whom swimming was
only endless, graceful undulation.
We each had to bring a strand of wrack in as proof,
and you coiled yours twice at the throat

for your swift, not-quite stylish crawl back. Later
you wore it unwound, an open garland, ends parallel
with the strings of your silver bikini bra, which I knew
undid by twin hooks and eyes at the back.

Sandy-legged, you sat on your heels the way girls can,
bursting the wet green bladders
like bubblewrap in your fingers, with
an odd intentness as if they'd annoyed you,

though perhaps it was me, because we never did
take the ultimate dare on that last night
before your holiday ended, and, though we wrote,
next summer everything was changed,

you 17 and with some athlete from the hire boats in tow,
that year's bikini yellow, with an octopus motif
on the mound of the crotch so daring I assumed only you
didn't understand quite how much.

You went to a white-tile university
and brought boyfriends home in the holidays. We met rarely,
though I had news of you through sedulous friendship
with your parents and brother,

no spy going to greater efforts of
self-assimilation, the camouflage of harmlessness,
for so little hard news and nothing of hope.
You married a boy from heathland Surrey,

the Betjeman belt, which girls have never stopped doing
as new money evicts old, and he actually was
that stereotype Something In The City,
tall, well-made and full of a remorseless bluster

which is a sign of lifelong immaturity.
I made an excuse on the day of the wedding,
though pitiably grateful to have been invited.
I gave you a pair of good tickets for *Cats*.

I had girlfriends, of course, but I chose them
for your eyes, as if jealousy might be possible
where there's no desire. I'd become
an emotional hermaphrodite, and I saw

your mother knew it in the sharp, bright compression
of her smile, and told you, who'd always known
how my islands were on the scale of sand-castles –
close to shore and too small to land on.

after Umberto Saba

Back in Arcadia

Back in Arcadia the trees
Are always in full leaf
Across the meadow, and in that light
Each leaf's defined; the fruit hangs
Clustered, gum-beaded-ripe,
Bowing the bough;
And every hillside has its echo.

Between the call and the echo
Is where the striped wasp buzzes;
And in that even more
Resonating interval
Between the echo and its answer
Pastoral is born, the ravaged fruit
Drops, the season's over.

Acknowledgements

Acknowledgements are due to the editors of the following publications where some of these poems first appeared:
The Amsterdam Review, The London Magazine, The Times Literary Supplement, Poetry Wales.

Thanks are due to Hélène Perrin for some corrections to the French.